BRAIN ACADEMY
Quests

MISSION FILE 5

Penny Hollander,
Jenny Plastow,
Louise Moore and
Richard Cooper

Consultant for NACE:
Sue Mordecai

nace

RISING★STARS

Rising Stars are grateful to the following people for their support in developing this series: Julie Fitzpatrick, Johanna Raffan and Belle Wallace

NACE, PO Box 242, Arnolds Way, Oxford, OX2 9FR
www.nace.co.uk

Rising Stars UK Ltd, 22 Grafton Street, London W1S 4EX
www.risingstars-uk.com

Every effort has been made to trace copyright holders and obtain their permission for the use of copyright materials. The authors and publisher will gladly receive information enabling them to rectify any error or omission in subsequent editions.

All facts are correct at time of going to press.

Published 2005
Reprinted 2005
Text, design and layout © Rising Stars UK Ltd

Editorial Consultant: Sue Mordecai
Design: Hart McLeod
Illustrations: Cover and insides – Sue Lee / Characters – Bill Greenhead
Cover Design: Burville-Riley

British Library Cataloguing in Publication Data.
A CIP record for this book is available from the British Library.

ISBN: 1-905056-36-2

Printed by Vincenzo Bona, Turin

CONTENTS

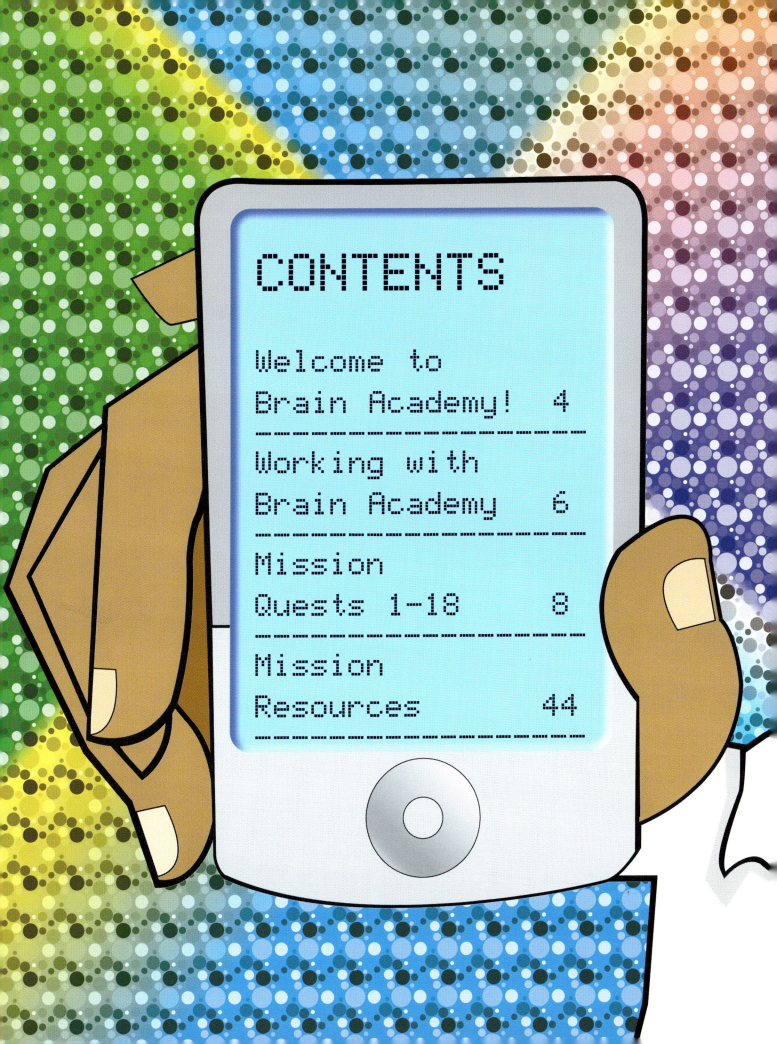

Welcome to Brain Academy!

Welcome to Brain Academy! Make yourself at home. We are here to give you the low-down on the organisation — so pay attention!

It's our job to help Da Vinci and his colleagues to solve the tough problems they face and we would like you to join us as members of the Academy. Are you up to the challenge?

Da Vinci

Da Vinci is the founder and head of the Brain Academy. He is all seeing, all thinking and all knowing – possibly the cleverest person alive. Nobody has ever actually seen him in the flesh as he communicates only via computer. When Da Vinci receives an emergency call for help, the members of Brain Academy jump into action (and that means you!).

Huxley

Huxley is Da Vinci's right-hand man. Not as clever, but still very smart. He is here to guide you through the missions and offer help and advice. The sensible and reliable face of Brain Academy, Huxley is cool under pressure.

Dr Hood

The mad doctor is the arch-enemy of Da Vinci and Brain Academy. He has set up a rival organisation called DAFT (which stands for Dull And Feeble Thinkers). Dr Hood and his agents will do anything they can to irritate and annoy the good people of this planet. He is a pain we could do without.

Hilary Kumar

Ms Kumar is the Prime Minister of our country. As the national leader she has a hotline through to the Academy but will only call in an extreme emergency. Confident and strong willed, she is a very tough cookie indeed.

General Cods-Wallop

This highly decorated gentleman (with medals, not wallpaper) is in charge of the armed forces. Most of his success has come from the help of Da Vinci and the Academy rather than the use of his somewhat limited military brain.

Mrs Tiggles

Stella Tiggles is the retired head of the Secret Intelligence service. She is a particular favourite of Da Vinci who treats her as his own mother. Mrs Tiggles' faithful companion is her cat, Bond… James Bond.

We were just like you once — ordinary schoolchildren leading ordinary lives. Then one day we all received a call from a strange character named Da Vinci. From that day on, we have led a double life — as secret members of Brain Academy!

Here are a few things you should know about the people you'll meet on your journey.

Echo the Eco-Warrior

Echo is the hippest chick around. Her love of nature and desire for justice will see her do anything to help an environmental cause – even if it means she's going to get her clothes dirty.

Maryland T Wordsworth

M T Wordsworth is the president of the USA. Not the sharpest tool in the box, Maryland prefers to be known by his middle name, Texas, or 'Tex' for short. He takes great exception to being referred to as 'Mary' (which has happened in the past).

Buster Crimes

Buster is a really smooth dude and is in charge of the Police Force. His laid-back but efficient style has won him many friends, although these don't include Dr Hood or the DAFT agents who regularly try to trick the coolest cop in town.

Serena

Serena is a new character to Brain Academy. A time-traveller, Serena knows all about what went on before – and a bit about the future too.

Sandy Buckett

The fearless Sandy Buckett is the head of the Fire Service. Sandy and her team of brave firefighters are always on hand, whether to extinguish the flames of chaos caused by the demented Dr Hood or just to rescue Mrs Tiggles' cat…

Victor Blastov

Victor Blastov is the leading scientist at the Space Agency. He once tried to build a rocket by himself but failed to get the lid off the glue. Victor often requires the services of the Academy, even if it's to set the video to record Dr Who.

Prince Barrington

Prince Barrington, or 'Bazza' as he is known to his friends, is the publicity-seeking heir to the throne. Always game for a laugh, the Prince will stop at nothing to raise money for worthy causes. A 'good egg' as his mother might say.

Working with Brain Academy

Do you get the idea? Now you've had the introduction we are going to show you the best way to use this book.

The Quest
This tells you what the quest is about.

MISSION QUEST 5:4

Rivers of information

Water, and how we move water about, is one of the most important conservation issues facing the world now. We have been asked to create the Brain Academy Encylopaedia of Ecology, which will be used by world leaders as they discuss how to take care of our world.

So, the Academy Questers have been recruited to write the section on rivers, Sandy.

But there are so many rivers around the world, Echo. Where do we start?

The Quest

Your quest is to find out as much as possible about one particular river. Try to organise your work so that you and your friends are working in pairs and that each pair is working on a different river so you can build up a bigger bank of data for the encyclopaedia. Choose your country first, then decide what information you want to include. The maximum number of words you can use is 200.

Research Area

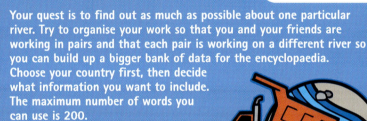

Atlases in your school or local library.
http://www.woodlands-junior.kent.sch.uk/Homework/Grivers.html#1

Visit your local riverside or canal with an adult to see what goes on there.

There is more information on pages 46–47.

Research Area
Da Vinci will give you some research tips before you start working on the brief.

Each mission is divided up into different parts.

No one said this was easy. In fact that is why you have been chosen. Da Vinci will only take the best and he believes that includes you. Good luck!

Each book contains a number of quests for you to take part in. You will work with the characters in Brain Academy to complete these quests.

The Brief

The Brief
This is where you try to complete the challenge.

- Use an atlas to find the country and the river you want to work on. In your 'Rivers File' notebook, write the name of the river and the countries it runs through. (There are likely to be several countries.)
- Where does the river start? Where does it reach the sea? Name the big towns and cities along its route.
- Look at the atlas and identify high land and low land. Use a highlighter pen to mark the place names in high areas, and a different colour for those in low land.
- Put the name of the river into Google and add 'dams'. You may be able to find out if any new dams have been built on your river. Write what you find in your notebook. Which country is the dam in? How will that affect other countries? What is the function of a dam?
- When you are ready to write your entry for the encyclopaedia, use report style (present tense). Set headings in bold to help you organise your text. Keep your entry below 200 words.

Rivers used to be the natural boundaries of countries. You might even live in an area that is named after a river, such as Newcastle-upon-Tyne or Henley-upon-Thames. Can you think of any more?

The longest rivers in the world are the Nile in Africa (4,145 miles or 6,670 km long) and the Amazon in South America (4,007 miles or 6,448 km long).

Da Vinci Files

You have created a basic database for your river.
- Now go to the library and see what you can find out about your river by using the reference guide.
- What local industries could affect that river? Is it polluted in some places? If so, what is causing the pollution? Are there still fish in the river? What could be done to prevent it becoming polluted?
- Look only at books published in the last five years, because information on rivers changes very quickly.
- Try to check your facts by using the search engines on the internet.

Da Vinci Files
These problems are for the best Brain Academy recruits. Very tough. Are you tough enough?

PS: See pages 44—47 for a useful process and hints and tips!

Up, up and away!

Victor, it appears that your space team is under attack from Dr Hood. We need to warn them of this or the space station will be destroyed.

We need to fly that information straight up to the team. Speed is of the essence, Da Vinci.

Don't worry. It's not exactly rocket science... err, well... I suppose it probably will be rocket science!

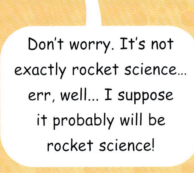

The Quest

Your quest is to design a rocket to carry the vital information up to the team before Dr Hood finds them. Your design must fly over 50 metres once launched and should fly as straight as possible.

Research Area

http://www.zingwing.com
http://www.trebuchet.com/plans

There is more information on pages 46–47.

The Brief

First, you must try to create a streamlined model that will fly at least 10 metres.

You should consider the following before starting to build the model:
- Design of the model – how can you make sure it flies the distance (and straight too!)?
- Materials you will use – think about the weight of the object and how it will fly through the air. Will paper or card be suitable?
- How easy it is to make – you must be able to get the materials and mould them into your design.

Next, design a launch system that will give your rocket the power to travel even further than 10 metres.

Think about these things:
- The rocket launch system must launch your own rocket, not another type of rocket, so design it around this.
- The rocket launch system could use elastic bands or a counter-weight system (a trebuchet).
- Draw the design first then build the model using junk modelling equipment.

Try launching it with different types of catapult, or vary the tension on the elastic.

Did you know that a spacecraft must reach a speed of about 17,500 mph (or 28,000 km/hr) in order to get into orbit! The booster rockets break away at a height of about 29 miles (47 km) and are recovered from the ocean to be used again.

Da Vinci Files

- Test a range of different elastic bands to see which is the most effective in launching the rocket.
- Have a class competition to see which rocket flies the furthest and which launcher is the best.

The 4R's

Da Vinci, it says in this article that schools are now teaching the 4R's in relation to caring for the environment. What on earth does that mean?

Well, the 3R's are 'reduce', 'recycle' and 'reuse'. The fourth R stands for responsibility: that means we all try to ensure that the first three R's happen, General.

And I thought the 3R's were reading, writing and arithmetic... it's all changed since I was a boy!

The Quest

As a member of the school council, you are going to organise a school project that will put the new 3R's into practice on a daily basis in school. Your quest is to present an action plan to the headteacher and school community, with practical ideas that can involve everyone and persuade them that they all have a responsibility for taking part in the project.

Research Area

http://www.recyclingconsortium.org.uk/news/index.htm
http://www.livingethically.co.uk

There is more information on pages 46–47.

The Brief

PLEASE RECYCLE!

- Research the 3R's and draw up a list of the various ways of carrying out each activity.
- Decide what is possible in school and make your choices. Find out some interesting facts and figures to support your choice.
- Write your action plan: what do you want everyone to do?

You will also need to think about:

- presenting your action plan to your class or group, and deciding which of the schemes should be put into practice;
- information to display in school about the 3R's, with examples of how to implement each one;
- providing a clear statement giving the reason why EVERYONE should be involved;
- appropriate collection points for items that could be reused or recycled;
- how you will gauge use of your recycling project.

Are there products that we use which cannot be recycled? If so, why not?

The richer and more developed a country is, the more waste it produces. Much of this waste is buried in areas called 'landfill sites', but what do you think will happen when these are completely full?

Da Vinci Files

- Find out from your local council how they manage the 3R's.
- Write an article for the school newspaper/newsletter about this and include your own opinions about whether they are doing enough and what else they could do.
- Make a simple information card for every student to take home, giving information on how and where to recycle.

Moving picture madness!

I've seen some of those very old films before, Victor. Don't they look rather strange and jerky?

Serena, the Brain Academy has had a request to set up a film archive. Collecting old films is one of Victor's hobbies, but he has also invented a way of showing how moving pictures work.

Well, when I have completed this device you will be able to see why!

The Quest

Your quest is to make a working model to show how still images combine to make movement. You should also write a recount of what you did in simple language so that it can be turned into captions that visitors to the film museum can read alongside the displayed model.

Research Area

http://www.abadie.co.uk/html/projects_flick.htm#
http://www.pixar.com/howwedoit/index.html

There is more information on pages 46–47.

The Brief

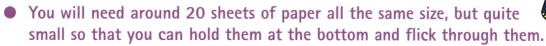

- You will need around 20 sheets of paper all the same size, but quite small so that you can hold them at the bottom and flick through them.
- On the top sheet, draw a person standing still.
- On the second, draw the same person in the same place on the paper, but beginning to put one foot forward as if walking.
- On the next, draw the person with a foot further forward, completing the step; on the next, beginning to move the other foot, and so on through the sequence. When you have finished your drawings hold the papers at the bottom and flick the pictures (or 'frames') so that your person appears to be walking.
- You may need to have more than one go at this to get it right, but when you are satisfied, staple the sheets together at the bottom and have a look at your friends' attempts!

- Your next job is to write a simple recount (past tense) of what you did. Remember to use words like first, next, then, in the end, so that your reader can easily find the way through the text.
- Type this up on the computer and put into a bold type. Break it up into short captions, so that it can be displayed in the museum, next to your model of the moving image.

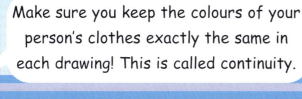

Make sure you keep the colours of your person's clothes exactly the same in each drawing! This is called continuity.

Next time you watch a cartoon film think about how many drawings it takes to move a single character. Can you see how it's done? Movies are filmed and played back at 24 frames per second and television shows display 30 frames per second!

Da Vinci Files

When you've made your model and written your recount, see if you can find out about other ways images were moved in the days before film was invented.

- See if you can find out anything about zoetropes; they spin still images to create movement.
- Create your own zoetrope using junk modelling equipment.

13

Rivers of information

Water, and how we move water about, is one of the most important conservation issues facing the world now. We have been asked to create the Brain Academy Encylopaedia of Ecology, which will be used by world leaders as they discuss how to take care of our world.

So, the Academy Questers have been recruited to write the section on rivers, Sandy.

But there are so many rivers around the world, Echo. Where do we start?

The Quest

Your quest is to find out as much as possible about one particular river. Try to organise your work so that you and your friends are working in pairs and that each pair is working on a different river so you can build up a bigger bank of data for the encyclopaedia. Choose your country first, then decide what information you want to include. The maximum number of words you can use is 200.

Research Area

Atlases in your school or local library.
http://www.woodlands-junior.kent.sch.uk/Homework/Grivers.html#1

Visit your local riverside or canal with an adult to see what goes on there.

There is more information on pages 46–47.

The Brief

- Use an atlas to find the country and the river you want to work on. In your 'Rivers File' notebook, write the name of the river and the countries it runs through. (There are likely to be several countries.)
- Where does the river start? Where does it reach the sea? Name the big towns and cities along its route.

- Look at the atlas and identify high land and low land. Use a highlighter pen to mark the place names in high areas, and a different colour for those in low land.
- Put the name of the river into Google and add 'dams'. You may be able to find out if any new dams have been built on your river. Write what you find in your notebook. Which country is the dam in? How will that affect other countries? What is the function of a dam?
- When you are ready to write your entry for the encyclopaedia, use report style (present tense). Set headings in bold to help you organise your text. Keep your entry below 200 words.

Rivers used to be the natural boundaries of countries. You might even live in an area that is named after a river, such as Newcastle-upon-Tyne or Henley-upon-Thames. Can you think of any more?

The longest rivers in the world are the Nile in Africa (4,145 miles or 6,670 km long) and the Amazon in South America (4,007 miles or 6,448 km long).

Da Vinci Files

You have created a basic database for your river.
- Now go to the library and see what you can find out about your river by using the reference guide.
- What local industries could affect that river? Is it polluted in some places? If so, what is causing the pollution? Are there still fish in the river? What could be done to prevent it becoming polluted?
- Look only at books published in the last five years, because information on rivers changes very quickly.
- Try to check your facts by using the search engines on the internet.

Heroes and villains!

Date: November 5th
Event: Bonfire party in the garden

That guy has gone off really well. No more than the real Guy Fawkes deserved. After all, he did try to blow up the Houses of Parliament.

Mamma mia! Not to an Italian Catholic girl like myself. The Catholics were brutally suppressed at the time and some people say that the whole thing was made up to discredit the Catholics. Guy Fawkes and his friends were set up!

Well, such violence should never be tolerated, Serena. He was a villain!

I think he was very brave and he stood up for what he thought was right. I say he was a hero!

Hmmm. It seems that history has more than one way of being viewed. It is all a matter of opinion. It depends on how you look at or read the evidence.

The Super Quest

Your challenge is to study 12 colourful and controversial characters from ancient history to the present day. You must look at as much evidence as you can and decide whether they were (or are) heroes or villains. Each decision must be backed up with your reasons.

Here are the chosen 12.

Name	Occupation	Mostly famous for...	Period of History
Guido Fawkes	Soldier, explosives expert	The Gunpowder Plot	The Stuarts – 1605
Crazy Horse	Native American warrior	Preserving the traditions and values of the Lakota way of life	The 'Indian Wars' – circa 1875
Enid Blyton	Author	Writing many children's books, including the 'Famous Five' series	The 1950s
Genghis Khan	Leader of the Mongol armies	Conquering most of the world!	13th Century
Sir Francis Drake	Tudor seafarer	Defeating the Spanish Armada	1588 and before
Emily Davison	Political activist	Grabbing the King's horse during the 1913 Derby at Epsom	1913 and before
Muhammad Ali	Sportsman	Being world heavyweight boxing champion	Circa 1960 to the present day
Spartacus	Gladiator	Leading the slaves' revolt	Circa 73 BC
Boudicca	Queen of the Iceni tribe in Ancient Britain	Resisting Roman rule	Circa 61 AD
Edward Teach	Professional pirate	His 'lost' treasure	The early 18th Century
Sir Arthur 'Bomber' Harris	Leader of Allied Bomber Command in WWII	'Carpet bombing' of Germany	The Second World War
Hernan Ferdinand Cortes	Spanish Conquistador	Defeating the Aztecs	Circa 1519

Research Area

You will need to have access to the school library and preferably your local library. There have been many books and biographies written about these people. Type their names into a search engine such as 'Google'. This will provide many links and lines of enquiry.

The Brief

- The result of this quest will form the basis of a display for your classroom.
- Prepare a personal profile for each of the characters. This could take the form of the following layout, which you could prepare on an index card for each person. You can work in pairs or groups and divide the characters between you.

NAME: _____

OCCUPATION: _____

BORN: _____

DIED: _____

MAJOR ACHIEVEMENTS: _____
_____

INTERESTING FACTS: _____
_____

I think this person is a HERO / VILLAIN.

My reasons are as follows:

- _____
- _____
- _____
- _____
- _____

I think Muhammad Ali is a villain. He threw his Olympic Gold Medal in a river!

I know WHY he did it. I think he is a hero!

The Brief

- Research each of the people in turn.
- Use as many different sources as you can. Don't get all your information from one website or book.
- Make notes about each person's achievements on a separate notepad before writing on the personal profiles.
- Your reasons must be backed up with evidence and opinion. Say 'WHY' you have reached your conclusions.
- Make a note of where you read the evidence.
- Mount all the heroes onto a large piece of display paper. They have entered your 'Hall of Fame'.
- Mount all the villains together on another display. They will be in your 'Hall of Shame'.
- Place each of the characters in one of the 'halls'. Find enough evidence so you are convinced you have placed them in the correct 'hall'.
- Discuss your choices, and your friends' choices. Are they the same? Compare your opinions.

Always have an open mind, my friends.

Incredibly, a sculpture that was started over 50 years ago, and is the size of a mountain, is still being made of one of these guys! Can you find out which one?

Da Vinci Files

Some people in history are made out to be horrible for political reasons. Over time these stories become 'facts'. A well known case for this is the way King Richard III is viewed by many. Shakespeare described him as a deformed, hunch-backed murderer.

He has also been described as 'a right high and mighty Prince' by the people of York. Why is there such a difference in the way he is spoken about?

Investigate his life and deeds. 'Hall of Fame' or 'Hall of Shame'?

School or 'l'ecole'?

The Brain Academy is adding to its website. I want to include a profile of each school where children are doing the Brain Academy quests. However, each profile has to be written in French!

Initialement, prendez-vous les informations, Da Vinci!

Then put it in a logical order, Serena!

Bonne chance!

The Quest

Your quest is to write a web page about your school – in French! You need to include plenty of facts about the school, but also say what you enjoy about being a student there and what makes your school different from others in the area.

Research Area

French dictionaries.
Web pages from other local schools.
French-speaking friends or relatives.

There is more information on pages 46–47.

The Brief

- Start by looking at some school websites. Notice how they are organised. What do you particularly like about what they have done?
- Next, collect facts about your school in a notebook. Organise them in a way that will help the reader to find out what they want to know, under headings. For example: buildings; number of pupils; number of classes; names of teachers; clubs; special facilities; school dinners; what the school does best. At this stage you only need notes, so use abbreviations!
- When you have your facts, use your notes to help you write a piece of text – in French – under each heading. As it is a report, make sure you use the present tense.
- Remember, a web page can be read by anyone looking for information. Would your page answer the questions of someone wanting to come to your school? Have you made it sound great? Keep each section short.

It is easier to write in French and check words as you go than to write in English and translate!

Do any of your classmates speak another language? Could they translate your web entry into their language too?

Da Vinci Files

In France, the schools have shorter holidays because they now only attend lessons for four days a week, with Wednesday being a day off.

- Hold a debate in your class on the topic 'Should we change to shorter holidays in order to have a four-day school week?'.
- Divide into two groups, prepare an argument either for or against the motion of longer terms/shorter holidays and make your case to the other half of the class.

Meat to eat?

Echo, why do you always have the vegeburger at the Brain Academy BBQ?

Because I'm a vegetarian, of course. I don't eat meat because I think it is wrong to harm animals.

Well, I think it's fine to eat meat. After all, cattle farms have existed for centuries for just that purpose.

The Quest

Your quest is to prepare a presentation for either Prince Barrington or Echo.
The presentation for the Prince must be in favour of eating meat.
The presentation for Echo must be in favour of vegetarianism.

Research Area

http://www.vegsoc.org is a good place to start if you need information about vegetarianism.
http://www.mlc.org.uk will provide you with lots of meaty facts.

There is more information on pages 46–47.

The Brief

After thinking about the issues and conducting your research, decide who you are going to support: the Prince or Echo. Your presentation needs to be biased and offer a persuasive argument. You should:

- Gather information from books, magazines and the internet.
- Ask your friends and family if they are vegetarian or meat-eaters. Ask them questions about their eating habits.
- Choose how you will present your argument. You can use one or more of the following: booklet, leaflet, letter, report or computer-generated article.
- Include a poster with diagrams to demonstrate at least one scientific fact.
- Cut out pictures and images from magazines to support your argument. Mount them with explanations for the viewer.
- Give the presentation a title.

I wonder how many types of meat are farmed in this country. Can you find out?

Do you think any animals are vegetarian? See what you can find out!

Jeff Giuliano was the actor who played a famous fast-food chain's clown mascot. After years of promoting burgers, he became horrified by the way animals were treated in the manufacture of the products and turned vegetarian!

Da Vinci Files

- Other countries eat different types of meat. The French eat horse and you can eat dog in South Korea.
- Investigate this further and prepare a mini-presentation on different meats eaten around the world.
- Research the cultural reasons why some religions eat or prepare meat in the way they do.

Intruder alert!

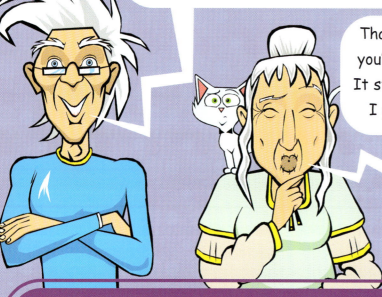

I've invented an early warning system so we will know when Dr Hood is nearing our headquarters, Huxley. In fact, he's coming now...

That's a funny door bell you've got there, Victor. It started ringing before I got to the building.

I think we need some smart thinking to sort this one out...

The Quest

Your quest is to create an early warning system for Da Vinci, so he can tell when Dr Hood is on his way. Once the system is installed, the Academy will be well prepared to deal with Dr Hood when he and his D.A.F.T. agents make another attempt to break into the building and steal their research.

Research Area

http://www.schoolscience.co.uk/content/3/physics/circuits/
http://www.howstuffworks.com/burglar-alarm1.htm

There is more information on pages 46–47.

The Brief

- First you need to draw a floorplan of the Brain Academy buildings and grounds.
- Now design a circuit with warning lights and buzzers that is activated by pressure sensors and light sensors. Use a push switch as a pressure sensor and work out how many doors and windows need to be covered.
- You need to provide Da Vinci's agents with transmitters to carry so they don't set the alarms off as well.
- Make sure you use the correct symbols for the circuits.
- Once you have designed your circuit, build it using lights, buzzers and sensors from your class resource box.

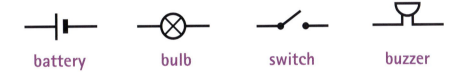

| battery | bulb | switch | buzzer |

Remember, never experiment with electricity at home or outside: it is VERY DANGEROUS.

Did you know that a bird sitting on an electric cable does not get an electric shock? This is because the bird is touching only one wire and its body does not complete an electric circuit.

Da Vinci Files

Test your circuit by getting Year 3 children to try to break in to your Brain Academy! Give them marks out of 10 for their efforts and make a reward badge for the person who gets the best score.

We'll always have Paris!

Some of the Brain Academy team are on holiday travelling in a camper van. They are touring around Paris and have stopped off for breakfast.

Who is going to buy us some goodies from the market?

I would, Huxley, but I've just spotted an injured pigeon.

This is ridiculous! Can't anybody speak the lingo? Leave it to me. Da Vinci old boy, can you get the Academy to send through some useful French phrases?

Er, I think the van needs some petrol, General.

Put your ear-piece in. I'll follow you on my web-cam and transmit what you have to say from here.

Humph! I'm too busy polishing my medals, Huxley!

Merci Monsieur. C'est un result!

The Super Quest

Your quest is to follow the Brain Academy team on their trip around Paris and help them with their French words and phrases. Da Vinci will transmit what you write to the team via their ear-pieces.

Research Area

A French/English dictionary.
A French phrase book.
Guidebooks to Paris: good ones include The Rough Guide, Lonely Planet, Time Out and the AA guide.
http://www.discover-paris.info is a useful website.

A very useful tool is the language option on Google. You should see it on the right of the screen. Click on 'Language Tools' and you will see a box which says 'Translate text'. Select 'English to French' and whatever you type in English will be translated into French! Double check with your phrase books as it can sometimes get it wrong.

There is more information on pages 46–47.

The Brief

You are going to create your own phrase book with different chapters for different situations. Use a piece of A4 paper for each one, writing your translations in the phrase book.

- Off to the market
- Tickets, please!
- Café Society
- Which way?
- Sight-seeing in Paris

You can bind all of the pages together to form a book. Illustrate the blank pages with scenes from Paris and Parisian landmarks.

I'm in the marketplace to buy some food. Transmit what I have to say.

Write these sentences in French:
- Four loaves of bread please.
- How much is that cheese?
- That cake looks good!
- Good morning Mrs Baker. Five croissants please.

 Now write out your favourite recipe for a French dish.

We need to travel on the Paris Metro. That's like the London Underground. Help!

Translate these sentences for the General:
- Five tickets for the Metro please.
- What time is the train?
- Where is the museum?
- How many stops are there?

Plan a journey from Notre Dame to the Eiffel Tower and make a map.

We've stopped for lunch in a cool little street café. Feed me some lines, quick!

Help Echo order lunch from the garçon:
- Hello, what is the dish of the day?
- Snails in a white wine and cream sauce? Very good!
- Tomato salad and chips, please.
- Five cups of coffee and the bill, please.

 Write shopping lists, in French, to suit Echo and Bazza's preferred diets.

We're lost again. I'll ask this policeman the way. Transmit to my ear-piece please.

Help Huxley get back on track.
- Excuse me Mr Policeman, where is the station?
- How can we get to the Eiffel Tower?
- How far is it to Notre Dame?
- Where are the public toilets? I am desperate!

Prepare a fact sheet about the Paris Metro.

I'm asking ze questions about ze famous sights in Paris. Vot must I say?

Help Victor overcome the language barrier!
- How tall is the Eiffel Tower?
- Was there really a hunchback of Notre Dame?
- The paintings in the gallery are beautiful. Who painted this one?
- That gentleman is very fashionable. Where can I buy a suit like that?

Take a place of interest and write an encyclopedia entry about it.

Da Vinci Files

- Practise speaking these lines and other phrases with your friends.
- You could role-play the Brain Academy characters and act out their adventures in Paris. Make up some other scenarios for them to be in. Using props such as tables, chairs, food and clothing will help you fit into role.

Au revoir, mes amis!

A sense of place

Water, wind, weather... issues about the environment arrive on the desks of the Brain Academy every day. But Da Vinci is keen to find out what the environment means to people, Hilary, and he needs something to brighten up his office...

That's right, Echo. The more we know about what people think, the better decisions we can make! Perhaps Da Vinci needs some artistic inspiration...

The Quest

Questers, your quest is to create a large piece of art for Da Vinci's office wall that illustrates what you feel is important about the environment. This is your chance to express what concerns you most about the world around you and to find really creative ways of showing it!

Research Area

Art books in your local library.
Visits to galleries and exhibitions.
Unusual materials that you can gather from natural sources around you, such as fallen leaves and acorns.

The Brief

- Start collecting ideas in a scrapbook that will help you to design a large frieze to go on Da Vinci's wall, expressing your concerns and feelings about the environment.
- The challenge here is to find materials that will give you opportunities to make something really different. While you are working on this challenge, notice what inspires you: is it the people around you, music, posters, buildings?
- Do you have ideas you already want to express? Does looking for materials, and finding something you like, help you?
- You might see an image somewhere around you, or in a magazine or newspaper, and think of other ways you could present it.
- Use this challenge to find out as much as you can about your own creative process, and keep a diary in your scrapbook of all the stages your thinking goes through. Then you'll be working just like one of the great artists!

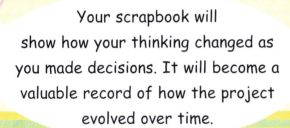

Your scrapbook will show how your thinking changed as you made decisions. It will become a valuable record of how the project evolved over time.

When Michelangelo painted the ceiling of the Sistine Chapel, it took four years to complete and he spent much of that time lying on his back on scaffolding to work on it! What is the largest piece of artwork you have seen?

Da Vinci Files

It's important in art to be able to create things, but you need to be able to read the images other people create as well.

- When you have made your work of art and completed your diary, go and look at the images the others have made.
- In another section of the diary, write your impressions of what they have done, and what you think they were trying to 'say' with their work. Interpreting the work of others is a good way to develop your own ideas.

Getting connected

Lots of problems in the world occur because we think of things only from our own point of view. Learning about how other people do things is one of the key challenges for the Brain Academy – that's why we spend time asking questions. The information that we gather makes lots of links in a big chain of knowledge.

I've always been keen on links between nations, Da Vinci, but I just don't know how to set them up!

Getting schools thinking is the best place to start, Tex! That's how we really create change!

The Quest

Your quest is to find out what your class thinks are the important issues in the world today. Then find out whether schoolchildren in another part of the country or world agree that those are the important issues too. Use the Research Area and Brief to put together a questionnaire and then map the results of your class and your 'twinned class' on a graph and present your findings to your school.

Research Area

This site will give you some ideas about how to construct market research questionnaires.

http://www.design-technology.info/KS3/Y9/page6.htm

There is more information on pages 46–47.

The Brief

Find out what your classmates think are the really important issues facing the world today.

- In groups, decide on the categories you are going to use for your research: The Third World? Poverty? Energy supply? Pollution? Will you cover UK or international issues? Compile a list of about 20 categories.
- Now with one partner, go through your list and make sure that none of your categories are duplicated.
- Next, decide how you will ask people to answer the questions you put to them. Some ideas are: 'On a scale of one to five, how important to you is...?' or 'How do you feel about...? Strongly/not at all.' Remember that you need to be able to categorise the response!

- Draft your questionnaire out on a piece of paper. Make any changes you think are needed, then type it on the computer. Print out enough copies for each person in your class. You could hand them out, but it's better to ask people the questions yourself if you can.
- Evaluate the responses. Make a graph to show how many people feel strongly about the different issues.
- Now, send the questionnaire to another school. You will finish up with two graphs, giving a comparison of how people feel about your list of issues. Summarise your findings on one side of A4 paper.

Set a return date when you send your questionnaire to your 'twin school' so that you can plan your presentation.

Make each question as focused as possible, ensuring that they are easy to understand and quick to answer.

Da Vinci Files

When you've completed the quest, you can use your questionnaire to survey different groups.

- What about asking your teachers? Or finding out what your parents think?
- In your group each person should take a role (your class, your twin school, your teachers, your parents) and present their view of the world to the class in just two minutes. You can use props to help you!

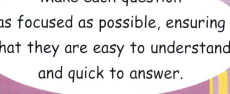

What did the Greeks ever do for us?

You know, Tex, the Ancient Greeks were the first great civilization.

Who were they, then, Serena? They sound really boring.

In a way, it's thanks to them that you became president. They invented democracy and were responsible for many things we take for granted today. You need to know these things so that you don't appear ignorant to the rest of the world.

The Quest

Your quest is to produce a handbook all about how we use Ancient Greek ideas today. For example, the men of Athens met to decide on laws for their community 2500 years ago: just like the way our parliament decides how our country should work for us today. These are things that Tex should be aware of, so your handbook will be a valuable resource for him in the White House.

Research Area

http://www.ancientgreece.com
http://www.historyforkids.org/learn/greeks/

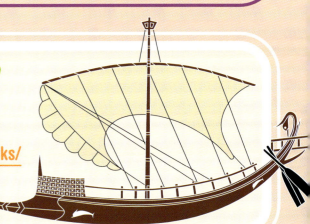

There is more information on pages 46–47.

The Brief

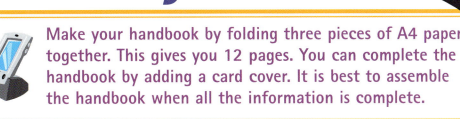

Make your handbook by folding three pieces of A4 paper together. This gives you 12 pages. You can complete the handbook by adding a card cover. It is best to assemble the handbook when all the information is complete.

Your handbook must contain these five chapters:
- Word and Alphabet
- Schools and Learning
- Architecture
- Democracy
- The Olympics

- Research each of the five areas. Include notes, articles, lists, examples, pictures and diagrams.
- Make up an interview with the Ancient Greek who interests you the most in your findings. Include it in the handbook.
- Give your completed handbook a title, contents page and an index.

Pythagoras could measure the height of a tall tree without climbing it. Can you find out how? (He didn't cut it down!)

Women weren't allowed to watch or compete in the Olympics because the male competitors were naked. Find out what Ancient Greek women did about this.

Da Vinci Files

The word 'academy' is an Ancient Greek word. The Academy was set up by Plato in around 350 BC. It was a peaceful garden of olive groves where people could stroll and discuss maths and philosophy. It was also a gymnasium!
- Research Plato's Academy on the internet.
- Take a piece of graph paper. Use what you find out to draw a plan of your own Academy.
- Keep to the Greek style and label it.

Flying high!

This traffic is a nightmare. I'm going to be late for my lecture at the Academy...

Really, Victor? Huxley may have some 'uplifting' news for you when you finally get here.

The Quest

Design a vehicle for use in the 21st Century. As you probably know, the world's oil reserves are running low and petrol will soon be exhausted. An alternative fuel source needs to be found before the planet grinds to a halt.

Alternative modes of transport and new sources of energy will be very important in the 21st Century.

Take a look at the 'Skycar' on this website – Victor won't believe it! http://www.moller.com

Research Area

Start by researching different sources of energy and modes of transport in an encyclopaedia and at these websites.

http://www.bbc.co.uk
http://www.popsci.com
http://www.dti.gov.uk/energy/

There is more information on pages 46–47.

The Brief

Stick to the following rules for your design.

- Your vehicle can be designed for use on land, sea, air or a combination of all three.
- It must carry at least two adults and a minimum of 500 kg cargo. It cannot be powered by fossil fuels.

Present your design in the following form.

- A labelled illustration of the vehicle from two different viewpoints on A3 paper.
- A description of at least 200 words on the features and how the vehicle is controlled.
- A summary of at least 200 words describing how your vehicle would revolutionise the transport system in the 21st Century.

Here are some questions to answer and points to consider if we're going to come up with a design good enough for Da Vinci.

- Consider the safety issues for the driver, passenger and the general public.
- What modifications, if any, will need to be made to existing transport systems before your vehicle can be used?
- Explain how your vehicle improves on existing inventions.
- Why would the general public choose your vehicle over traditional forms of transport? Think of the pros and cons and try to address the arguments for each.

Da Vinci Files

Now take your quest to the next level and beyond.

Produce a word-processed report on your invention. It should include information about safety issues, operating instructions and the special features of the vehicle. You can also use pictures.

Eyes everywhere!

It's impossible, Serena! We need eyes in the back of our heads to spot what that Dr Hood is going to get his D.A.F.T. agents to do next.

It's not impossible, Buster. We just need a little help to complete one of Victor's incredible designs. I've seen this kind of thing on my time travels...

OK, Serena, I'll stop feeling down if this invention can pick up my arrest rates!

The Quest

Your quest is to design a set of tools to help Buster Crimes and his police squad see behind their backs and around corners. The periscope is the best version of this. It was first seen in the 1430s to help people see over the heads of crowds at religious festivals.

Research Area

Look at these websites to find out about reflections and how to use them to see round corners.

http://www.bbc.co.uk/schools/scienceclips/ages/10_11/see_things.shtml
http://www.exploratium.edu/science_explorer/periscope.html

There is more information on pages 46–47.

The Brief

Design and make at least one of these instruments:
- a tool for looking over the top of high walls;
- a tool for looking down into tall chimneys;
- a tool to look behind your back.

- Think about whether you are going to have to look forward, backwards, up or down and then draw a diagram to show how the light must travel.
- You will need to have access to some reflective materials to make these work.
- Use modelling materials to build your instrument and try it out!
- Prepare a set of instructions on how to use your gadget once it is working successfully. You may need to build more than one prototype to get it right!

Submarines use periscopes to see over the surface of the waves when they are submerged. According to legend, the first submarine was used in battle by Alexander the Great in 332 BC. Find out more about how this could have worked.

Da Vinci Files

Write a script for a radio or television advert to sell your device. What could it be used for? How easy is it to use? Would you use it at home, outside or in industry?
- Remember to keep the script short as you may only have a couple of minutes to get your audience's attention.
- Perform your advert and record it using a tape recorder or digital camera.

Pet rescue!

Those dastardly D.A.F.T. agents have stooped so low as to kidnap Mrs Tiggles' cat, James Bond! The poor pussy was napping in the garden when he was bundled into a sack and whisked off before he could say 'Meeowwuch!'

Luckily, Mrs Tiggles saw the whole thing through the window but was unable to stop the cat-napping. Like a flash (well, quite quickly) she phoned Buster Crimes, whose plucky officers caught the cat burglars with fur on their fingers – but there was no sign of James!

After being tickled mercilessly the thieves have confessed that, in their hurry to escape the police, they dropped James down a disused mine-shaft!

The Quest

James's faint cries can be heard but there is no way down the mine-shaft to rescue him. The only way in is through a narrow access tunnel which joins the shaft, which is too small for anyone to fit through because of previous roof collapses. James is too scared to move, so a special cat-rescue vehicle is needed to carry the mistreated moggy to safety. It's time to call the Academy!

Da Vinci, can you help poor James?

Not to worry, Mrs T. I think Victor and our friends have been busy in the research lab and may have the purrfect solution for rescuing our favourite feline.

Research Area

Try looking at these websites and books for information about controllable vehicles. Ask your teacher for access to all the construction kits you may have in school. There is more information on pages 46–47.

Go to **www.lego.com** and click on the technic section. Explore the website at **www.youngeng.org**

Books

Visit the Amazon store at **www.amazon.co.uk** and enter 'construction toys' in the search box. There are a number of interesting titles available.

Look at some model controllable vehicles.
Think about the following:
- How are they powered?
- How are the wheels driven?
- Where are the switches and how do they work?
- What are the similarities and the differences between the vehicles?
- How are the different parts joined together?

Record your findings by making some labelled drawings of the best models.

CONTINUED ➡

41

The Brief

Your brief is to design a controllable vehicle which would be able to rescue the cat, James Bond, from the end of the 5-metre long tunnel.

For the mission to be a success and a 'cat-astrophy' to be avoided, the vehicle will need to do these tasks:

- travel forward a distance of 5 metres;
- stop and reverse 5 metres (James will clamber on by himself);
- carry a weight of at least 3 kilograms (he is a 'well-looked-after' cat).

In order to achieve this it will help if you:

- Use a construction kit to make a working model of a vehicle with a motor. How can you make it go faster or slower?
- Revise your work on circuits. Build a motor into a circuit. How can the direction of the motor be changed? Attach a small pulley to the motor spindle and use an elastic band to make a belt drive. Place the belt around another pulley which is fixed to an axel held firmly in a box. Is the belt turning quickly or slowly? How can you change the speed?
- Think about the size and shape of the vehicle. You can build frames from balsa wood or plastic and metal construction kits. Will it be strong enough? Will the motor be powerful enough to move the weight?

Here is a list of suitable tools and equipment:

Batteries	Connector strips	Switches
Motors	Axels	Wheels
Wire	Motor mounting clips	Elastic bands
Pulleys	Balsa wood	Popular construction kits
Glue	Screwdrivers	Tape

Da Vinci Files

You should have enough information to build your vehicle to rescue that pussy-cat.

You could follow this formula:

- Recap on the purpose of your vehicle.

- Work in pairs to discuss your ideas.

- Make labelled plans of your design.

- List all the materials and equipment.

- Show your designs to your teacher before you start.

- Test and adapt your model as you go. What can you do to make it better?

- Does your model work? Would it be able to rescue James (by completing the three points in the brief)?

- Can you suggest any improvements?

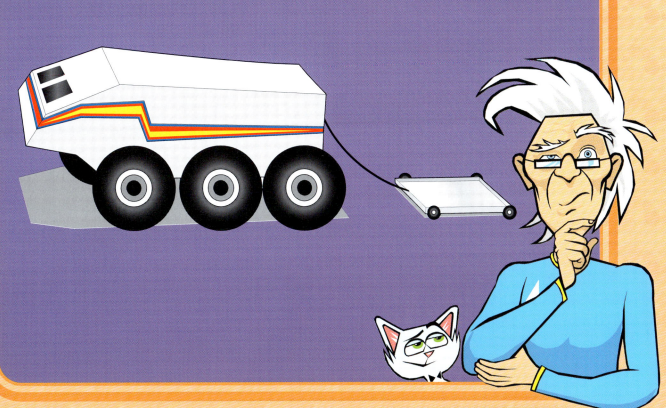

The TASC Problem Solving Wheel

TASC: Thinking Actively in a Social Context

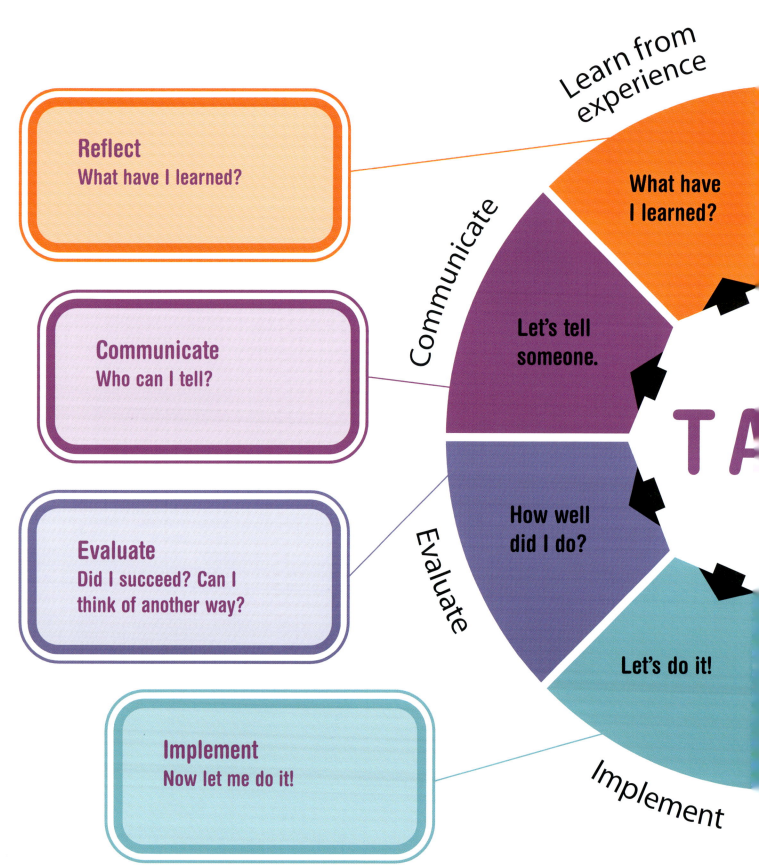

Reflect
What have I learned?

Communicate
Who can I tell?

Evaluate
Did I succeed? Can I think of another way?

Implement
Now let me do it!

Learn from experience

What have I learned?

Communicate

Let's tell someone.

How well did I do?

Evaluate

Let's do it!

Implement

TA

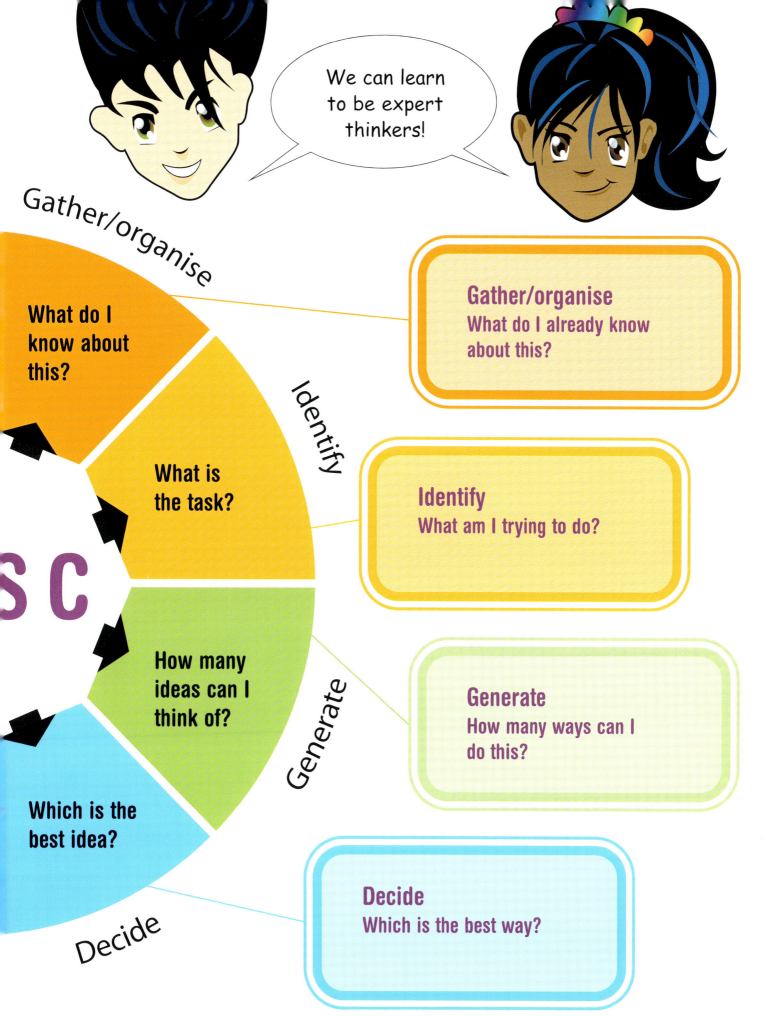

TASC: Thinking Actively in a Social Context © Belle Wallace 2004

The Quest Online Library

Mission Quest 5.1
For more information try:
http://starchild.gsfc.nasa.gov

Mission Quest 5.2
For more information try:
http://www.northmoortrust.co.uk
http://www.bbc.co.uk/scotland/education/sysm/eco/eco_friendly.shtml

Mission Quest 5.3
For more information try:
http://www.randommotion.com/html/zoe.html
Look at your favourite animated film and try to see how they made it happen. New movies such as Finding Nemo, Shrek and The Incredibles are created with computers, but older films such as Snow White and the Seven Dwarves were made with up to one million hand-drawn cels!

Mission Quest 5.4
For more information try:
http://www.kids.net.au/encyclopedia-wiki/ri/River

Mission Quest/SUPERQUEST 5.5–5.6
For more information try:
http://www.guy-fawkes.com
http://www.bbc.co.uk/history/historic_figures/#
Film: Spartacus (Director: Stanley Kubrick, 1960)

Mission Quest 5.7
For more information try:
http://www.bbc.co.uk/schools/primaryfrench/
Book: French for Beginners (Usborne, ISBN 0746000545)

Mission Quest 5.8
For more information try:
Book: Vegetarian Cooking (Usborne, ISBN 074603038X)

Mission Quest 5.9
For more information try:
Books: Look at the Horrible Science series (Scholastic Hippo), which has books on Electricity, Light and Sounds or Electricity (DK Eyewitness Books, ISBN 0756613884)

Mission Quest/SUPERQUEST 5.10–5.11

For more information try:

http://www.pdictionary.com/french/

Book: Essential French Phrasebook and Dictionary (Usborne, ISBN 0746041691)

Mission Quest 5.12

For more inspiration, look up works of art by Andy Goldsworthy, a British environmental artist and Christo and Jeanne-Claude, two artists who wrap landmarks in huge pieces of cloth to show how the environment can be changed through art.

Mission Quest 5.13

For more information try:

http://www.makepovertyhistory.org/

http://www.eastbourne.gov.uk/Your_Environment/Pollution/index.asp

Mission Quest 5.14

For more information try:

http://www.bbc.co.uk/schools/ancientgreece/main_menu.shtml

Book: Horrible Histories: The Groovy Greeks (Scholastic Hippo, ISBN 0590132474)

Mission Quest 5.15

For more information try:

http://www.cornwallis.kent.sch.uk/intranet/subjects/science/renew/alternative_energy.html

http://www.consumereducation.org.uk/environment/english/energy/02.htm

Mission Quest 5.16

For more information try:

http://en.wikipedia.org/wiki/Periscope

Mission Quest/SUPERQUEST 5.17–5.18

For more information look at the amazing Meccano models on display at the South East London Meccano society website: http://www.selmec.org.uk

nace

What is NACE?

NACE is a charity which was set up in 1984. It is an organisation that supports the teaching of 'more-able' pupils and helps all children find out what they are good at and to do their best.

What does NACE do?

NACE helps teachers by giving them advice, books, materials and training. Many teachers, headteachers, parents and governors join NACE. Members of NACE can use a special website which gives them useful advice, ideas and materials to help children to learn.

NACE helps thousands of schools and teachers every year. It also helps teachers and children in other countries, such as America and China.

How will this book help me?

Brain Academy books challenge and help you to become better at learning by:
* Thinking of and testing different solutions to problems
* Making connections to what you already know
* Making mistakes and learning from them
* Working with your teacher, by yourself and with others
* Expecting you to get better and to go on to the next book
* Learning skills which you can use in other subjects and out of school.

We hope that you enjoy the books!

Write to **RISING STARS** and let us know how the books helped you to learn and what you would like to see in the next books.

Rising Stars Ltd, 22 Grafton Street, London W1S 4EX